YELLOWSTONE
and
Grand Teton National Parks

GALLERY BOOKS
An Imprint of W. H. Smith Publishers Inc.
112 Madison Avenue
New York City 10016

This edition first published in U.S.
in 1991 by Gallery Books,
an imprint of W.H. Smith Publishers, Inc.
112 Madison Avenue, New York, New York 10016

ISBN 0-8317-0256-7

Printed and bound in Spain

For rights information about the photographs in
this book please contact:

The Image Bank
111 Fifth Avenue, New York, NY 10003

Producer: Solomon M. Skolnick
Writer: Marcus Schneck
Design Concept: Lesley Ehlers
Designer: Ann-Louise Lipman
Editor: Joan E. Ratajack
Production: Valerie Zars
Photo Researcher: Edward Douglas
Assistant Photo Researcher: Robert V. Hale
Editorial Assistant: Carol Raguso

Title page: *Yellowstone and Grand Teton national parks are home to an awe-inspiring array of nature's wildest features. The Grand Canyon of the Yellowstone, carved deep into the earth by the constant action of the Yellowstone River, is just one of countless such spectacles.* Opposite: *Hot springs, such as these in Yellowstone's West Thumb Geyser Basin, are closely related to geysers. Unlike geysers, however, hot springs do not erupt because their underground channels are not tight and restricted.*

Yellowstone and Grand Teton national parks—set in the center of the largest intact, Temperate Zone ecosystem on Earth and encompassing a total of 8.5 million acres or 13,280 square miles—together make up the largest and most primitive wild region left in the contiguous U.S. The erupting power of Old Faithful, the unexpected grizzly bear on the trail ahead, the huge herds of elk and bison, and the incredible majesty of the Grand Teton peaks at sunrise all conspire to remind visitors that there are still strong and wild forces at play here. Despite the roads, guardrails, and buildings, one has the feeling that the Earth is untamed, that perhaps humans are not totally in control.

Millions of visitors stream along the roadways in these parks every year, most experiencing the wilderness without ever straying far from the developed areas. The large animals that attract so much of the visitors' attention graze right at roadside. The breathtaking geologic forces—the geysers, the majestic mountains, the rivers—can be seen close up during a walk on well-developed trails. World-famous rivers and streams—the Madison, the Firehole, the Gibbon, the Snake—have similarly easy access. Grand hotels, ballrooms, and fine dining await at major junctions in and near the parks.

Yellowstone holds many surprises, even for those who have visited many times. Fishing Cone, an underwater geyser in Yellowstone Lake, is part of the West Thumb Geyser Basin.

For more adventurous visitors, Yellowstone and Grand Teton national parks offer a back-country brimming with forests, meadows, and unparalleled vistas. More than 1,200 miles of marked hiking trails cut through the two parks.

The 3,472-square-mile Yellowstone National Park became the world's first national park on March 1, 1872, when it was established by Congress. The name was taken from the moniker *roche jaune* (yellow stone) that French Canadian traders and trappers had given to the region's river. (The coloring is caused by underground hot water dissolving hardened lava.)

Although the final action of designating and protecting the park was left to the bureaucrats in Washington, the concept had first emerged a few years earlier among members of the exploring Washburn-Langford-Doane Party. As these adventurers sat around their campfire at the base of what today is known as National Park Mountain, they had mulled over the many uses to which the wonders they had

Preceding page: *Old Faithful is neither the largest nor the most regularly erupting of Yellowstone's geysers. However, it does erupt every 45-90 minutes without fail and has become the most famous geologic feature on the face of the Earth.* This page, top to bottom: *Grotto Geyser erupts steadily for six to 10 hours at a time, but its splashes rarely rise more than a dozen feet into the air. The strange "broken" cone of Grotto Geyser is the result of geyserite deposited on the trunks of once-living trees near the geyser. The geysers, hot springs, fumeroles, and mudpots of Yellowstone are all geothermal features caused by water coming into contact with the molten rock that lies only three to five miles under the region's surface.*

When Great Fountain Geyser begins to erupt, its crater fills with water and then overflows. Eventually, spouts burst through the surface of the water, sometimes rising as high as 150 feet. Below: *The late afternoon sun casts a red-orange glow across mud terraces at Midway Geyser Basin.*

Dead, dried tree trunks in Biscuit Geyser Basin exhibit the effects of standing in the mineral-rich waters of the area. Below: The original color of Morning Glory Pool was that of the flower for which it is named, but the popular attraction has been victimized by tons of coins, trash, and debris thrown into it. As a result of this pollution, brown and green algae have spread.

Above: *The run-off water from Fountain Paint Pots supports blooms of many types of algae year-round, creating a pallet of colors downstream as well as in the geysers.* Opposite: *Clouds of steam fill the air around Midway Geyser Basin as the run-off from the geysers drains into Firehole River.* Overleaf: *When the members of the Washburn, Langford, and Doane expedition (one of the first formal expeditions into the region) wrote about the features of Yellowstone, their diaries were filled with such descriptions as, "greatest wonders on the continent." The geyserite cone at Castle Geyser (right) is the largest in Yellowstone. Castle may be one of the very oldest geysers in the park.*

observed could be put. The altruistic idea of preserving the spectacular site for all citizens quickly gained acceptance throughout the group and then spread across the country.

Yellowstone was under the regulation and protection of the U.S. Cavalry from 1886 to 1916, when the National Park Service was created. Park headquarters today are housed partly in what was then Fort Yellowstone at Mammoth. At its peak in 1910, the fort was garrisoned with 324 soldiers.

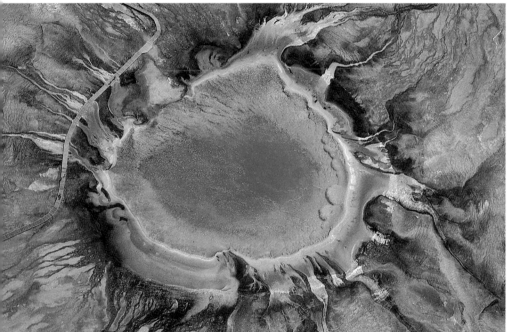

Grand Teton National Park received its first official protection in 1929, when it encompassed only the Teton mountains and a thin wisp of land pockmarked with piedmont lakes. In 1950, the park was expanded to include Jackson Hole National Monument, first established in 1943. All together, the park today is nearly 500 square miles, roughly 38 miles long by 24 miles wide.

Connecting Yellowstone and Grand Teton is the seven-mile-long John D. Rockefeller, Jr. Memorial Parkway, established by an act of Congress on August 25, 1972. Dedicated to its namesake for his contributions to national park conservation, the parkway forms a corridor from Grand Teton to Yellowstone between Targhee and Teton national forests.

This page, top to bottom: *Oblong Geyser, one of 65 major geysers in Yellowstone's Upper Geyser Basin, erupts every three to 18 hours, sending a spout of water 20 to 40 feet into the air. Algae populations are responsible for many of the colors in Yellowstone's geothermal features. Grand Prismatic Spring, which measures 370 feet in diameter, is the largest hot spring in Yellowstone.* Opposite: *The number of Yellowstone's thermal features has been estimated at more than 10,000—more than all the others on Earth combined.*

Above: *Steamboat Geyser once carried the most potential power of any geyser in Yellowstone. Its spout shot 400 feet into the air when it was in its major phase of activity many years ago.* Opposite: *Visitors often know they are approaching a geyser basin well before the park signs or the thermal features themselves are visible because the sulphurous odor emitted by a geyser basin can travel great distances.*

At first glance, a thermal basin appears to be virtually lifeless, with only scattered, struggling vegetation, but on closer inspection, a plethora of tiny animals and plants show their special adaptations to life in this environment. Below: Porcelain Basin, part of Norris Geyser Basin, is named for the porcelain-like gray and white geyserite that has formed at many of its thermal features.

The two parks are a veritable treasure chest of awe-inspiring geologic phenomena.

Yellowstone is home to approximately 10,000 hydrothermal features, the largest gathering of such features anywhere on Earth. The area boasts nearly 250 geysers and one of Earth's largest calderas (a large crater formed by volcanic explosion and collapse) which measures nearly 30 miles by 40 miles.

Among all these natural wonders is perhaps the world's most famous geologic feature: Old Faithful. While it's not the largest, highest, or even the most regular geyser in Yellowstone, it has received more attention than all the others combined. Old Faithful erupts 21 to 23 times every day at intervals ranging from 32 to 120 minutes. The spout averages about 130 feet in height, but has been recorded at more than 180 feet.

The most powerful geyser in the park, Steamboat, is less well known. When Steamboat erupts, which it has done only a few times in the past 20 years, it expels a spout 300 to 350 feet into the sky.

Some groups of Native Americans avoided this region of rumbling, hissing, spitting ground, fearing that it was the playground of evil spirits. The first explorers of European descent were similarly frightened by what they found. Pierre-

Above: *An extinct geyser, Liberty Cap stands as a pillar of inactive, solidified geyserite near Mammoth Hot Springs.* Right: *Bleached and dried trees are coated with minerals that have been spewed into the waters from the nearby geysers.*

Sheepeater Cliffs, a series of five- and eight-sided posts formed from cooled molten volcanic rock, marks the area in northwest Yellowstone where the peaceful Sheepeater Indians once lived. **Below:** *The calcite terraces of Mammoth Hot Springs appear to be locked in the grip of winter's ice even in the heat of summer.* **Opposite:** *Much of the terrace area of Mammoth Hot Springs is covered in travertine, a white form of calcium carbonate that originates in underground limestone.*

Preceding page: *Roosevelt Arch, which spans the North Entrance Road into Yellowstone, was dedicated in 1903 by President Theodore Roosevelt. The sagelands in this area are prime spots for pronghorn antelope watching.* This page, right: *Blacktail Plateau Drive, atop Blacktail Deer Plateau in northern Yellowstone, provides a quiet drive amid fields of wildflowers, away from the crowds of the peak season.* Below: *Several deep gorges have been cut through Blacktail Deer Plateau by raging rivers such as Lava Creek.*

Jean de Smet, a Jesuit missionary, described it as "the abode of evil spirits...a kind of hell." However, some Native Americans, including the Shoshone, and later European adventurers were drawn here in pursuit of the abundant game.

All this hydrothermal magnificence is the result of cataclysmic volcanic eruptions of some 600,000 years ago. Heat from the same molten rock reservoir that produced those massive eruptions remains relatively close to the Earth's surface today, sustaining the hot water and steam phenomena.

While the geysers may be the most awesome display of the Earth's internal forces, few of Yellowstone's hydrothermal features have the sheer grace and beauty of Mammoth Hot Springs. Hot water filled with minerals from deep beneath the Earth's crust emerges on the surface in this northern part of Yellowstone, building tier upon tier of cascading, pastel-hued, terraced stone. It's a continuing process, with another two tons of limestone forming at these springs every day.

Preceding page: *Petrified tree stumps can be found in a few locations in northern Yellowstone.
At one time, before collectors removed them, many more of these remnants from the redwood
forests of millions of years ago abounded. Above: A solitary angler fishes at the base of Gibbon
Falls, where waters from the Gibbon River cascade down an 84-foot drop.*

Different aquatic forces have carved still another of Yellowstone's magnificent geologic wonders. The Grand Canyon of the Yellowstone River is 24 miles of golden-hued cliffs headed by thunderous Lower Falls, which is twice the height of Niagara Falls. Artist Point, one of the park's most scenic views, stands at the top of a sheer drop of nearly 700 feet to the bottom of the canyon.

The volcanic beginnings of the region can also be seen in the northern part of the park, in a small, petrified forest. The trees there were turned to stone by volcanic eruptions and silica-rich waters some 50 million years ago.

Not to be outdone, Grand Teton National Park offers its own brand of spectacular geography. The tallest peak in the Teton Range is Grand Teton, towering 13,770 feet above sea level. It is joined by seven other summits in the park, each rising to more than 12,000 feet.

Preceding page: Rainbows often appear in photographs taken of Tower Falls, which drops 132 feet from amid the "towers" of volcanic rock for which it is named. This page, above: The yellow-colored rock seen here in the walls of the Grand Canyon of the Yellowstone inspired the name of this region. Below: The Grand Canyon of the Yellowstone stretches for 24 miles through the north-central part of the park, dipping from 800 to 1,200 feet in depth.

Above: *As the Yellowstone River courses through the Grand Canyon of the Yellowstone, it falls over two waterfalls and drops a total of 417 feet.* Opposite: *The Lower Falls area of the Grand Canyon of the Yellowstone can be viewed in all its breathtaking, 308-foot-deep glory from trails on either side of the canyon.* Overleaf: *At Upper Falls, the Yellowstone River changes from the gentle meander of the Hayden Valley to the roaring gush of the Grand Canyon of the Yellowstone.*

Above: *A rainbow forms over a grass- and shrub-covered ridge in the Hayden Valley, which was once at the bottom of a much larger Yellowstone Lake.* Opposite: *The Hayden Valley is one of Yellowstone's prime wildlife viewing areas: Large herds of bison can be seen at close range. Moose are common. Grizzly bears are often sighted from the roadway, and waterfowl abound in the valley's many wetlands.*

While the unique geology of the region gives it its form and structure, it is the wildlife that truly gives the parks their character. More than 60 species of mammals, 200 species of birds, 11 species of fish, five species of reptiles, and four species of amphibians make their homes in the region. But it is the few mega-fauna (the naturalist's name for large animals) species—elk, bison, moose, mule deer, pronghorn antelope, bighorn sheep, coyote, grizzly bear, and black bear—that draw and rivet the visitor.

Elk are by far the most abundant of these mega-fauna. The summer ranges of five major herds, totalling more than 30,000 animals, overlap in Yellowstone and another 3,000 head spend the summer in Grand Teton. The northern Yellowstone herd, more than 20,000 head in some years, is thought to be the largest migratory elk herd in North America. Additionally, thousands of the big animals move through Grand Teton each spring and fall as part of their migration to the National Elk Refuge, beyond the southern boundary of the park.

The 25,000-acre refuge provides a winter residence for an average annual herd of 7,500 animals. They remain there for about six months, receiving supplemental feeding of seven to

This page, top to bottom: *Pellets of hot mud are spit from mudpots, which are common in several parts of Yellowstone. The many mudpots, such as those of the Mud Volcano area, are formed where hot water mixes with clay and minerals in the soil. At Mud Volcano, the most ominous of Yellowstone's thermal areas, the ground is in a constant state of turmoil and the "rotten egg" smell is pervasive.*

eight pounds of pelleted alfalfa per animal per day for about two and one-half of those months. Horse-drawn sleighs carry visitors into the refuge daily during this period for close-up viewing of the herds. The local Boy Scout troop raises money by selling the antlers the bulls shed before leaving the refuge.

Bison herds likewise are a common sight throughout the region. Their population has been increasing steadily for several years, to the point that Montana game officials now allow limited hunter harvests along the northern Yellowstone boundary. A total of 568 bison were taken by hunters in 1989.

An estimated 3,000 of the big, shaggy creatures roam Yellowstone today. Only in the seclusion and protection of the park have wild bison, which inhabited the region since before recorded history, continued to exist. The current population is the result of two bloodlines: the original native bison of the region and the plains bison that were introduced in 1902.

Mule deer, moose, and pronghorn antelope are common in the region, respectively seen most often in the forested expanses, swampy openings, and sagebrush areas. Coyote can be seen stalking their rodent prey any morning or evening, and even during

Above: *The yellow-bellied marmot, also known as the rockchuck and mountain marmot, is common among the rocky slopes in the Old Faithful and Canyon areas of Yellowstone. The rodents hibernate through the winter.* Right: *Pikas are regular sights on talus slopes throughout Yellowstone and Grand Teton. Each summer this small relative of the rabbit stores huge amounts of grass and other vegetation in dried haystacks for winter use.*

Above: *Large herds of elk can be viewed at close range in many parts of Yellowstone and Grand Teton, particularly in early fall and winter. The National Elk Refuge, where thousands of the huge deer spend each winter, is adjacent to the southeastern border of Grand Teton.*

Right: *Although the roadside beggars of decades past are gone, black bears are still regularly sighted in both parks. They are much smaller than grizzlies and lack the shoulder hump.* Below: *Almost every visitor to Yellowstone hopes to catch a glimpse of a member of one of the last remaining wild populations of grizzly bear in the contiguous 48 states. The bears are generally retiring and keep to the wildest sections of the park.*

Bighorn sheep are most often seen in flocks of several dozen at Mount Washburn in Yellowstone. At its highest point, Mount Washburn is 10,243 feet above sea level. Below: Coyotes prowl through sageland and scrubland in Yellowstone and Grand Teton. Opposite: Mule deer, such as this prime buck with its antlers in velvet, are most often spotted at the edges of thick forests throughout the region.

The pronghorn antelope (left) is capable of speeds of 60 miles per hour over short distances. The Tower Falls, North Entrance, and Mammoth areas of Yellowstone, and Antelope Flat and the Jackson Airport area of Grand Teton, are prime viewing areas. Bison (right) may be seen at almost anytime anywhere throughout the parks, although large herds generally remain close to the grassy river valleys. Below: The moose is the largest member of the deer family, with adult bulls topping the scales at more than 1,000 pounds. Both parks have large populations of the animals.

the midday hours, in most open areas of the parks.

Yellowstone's bighorn sheep population was decimated by an outbreak of pinkeye in 1980–81 that killed an estimated 60 percent of the herd. Since then, however, the animals have staged a comeback and nearly 300 have been counted in recent censuses.

About 200 grizzly bears live in the region, comprising about a fifth of the estimated 1,000 that still survive in the wild in the 48 contiguous states. These scattered bears are the remnants of the population of 100,000 or more believed to have roamed most of the North American continent before the coming of European explorers.

Recent research has indicated that the Yellowstone region's grizzly population is expanding both its numbers and its range, occupying new habitats in densities not seen since the observations began in 1959.

The black bear, the grizzly's smaller cousin, is similarly flourishing in the vastness of this region. The population is estimated to be several times that of the grizzly, although the black bear is seen less often because of its penchant for dense forest areas far from the sites of human activity.

This page, top to bottom: *Although beavers are not uncommon in the two national parks, their numbers have declined in recent years because of the dwindling stands of aspen and willow trees, which are the prime food sources of the large rodent. Beavers, which have the well-deserved reputation of being nature's engineers, are constantly at work building and maintaining their dams, lodges, and food stores. Although few visitors actually get to see them, river otters are residents of all the major rivers of this region, particularly the Snake and Yellowstone rivers.*

Above: *A trumpeter swan assumes its defensive posture when any creature approaches its nest on the Madison River in Yellowstone.* Opposite: *Yellowstone provides one of the few remaining active nesting sites in the U.S. for the rare trumpeter swan.*

Above: *The only breeding colony of white pelicans in any national park exists on Yellowstone Lake. The birds can be seen diving into the lake's waters to secure their meals of fish.* Opposite: *Yellowstone Lake, measuring 20 miles long by 14 miles wide, is North America's largest lake occurring at such a high elevation—7,733 feet above sea level.* Overleaf: *Emigrant Peak towers over the Yellowstone River near the northernmost boundary of Yellowstone in Montana.*

Preceding page: *Fires raced through nearly a million acres of Yellowstone in the summer of 1988, burning huge tracts of forest. Total devastation, however, was limited to only a few small spots.* This page, right: *More than 25,000 firefighters, as many as 9,000 at a time, were involved in the battle against the fires of 1988.* Below: *Firefighters moved up a slope toward the fireline as another lodgepole pine exploded into flame.*

This is quite different from the situation of just a few years ago. Huge traffic jams often resulted as visitors stopped their cars to feed the bruins through the windows or at even closer range. Property damage, injury to humans, bear-car collisions, and the almost constant need for removal of "problem" bears from the population were the results of this unnaturally close human-bear contact.

In the mid-1960's, park administrators began the long and sometimes painful task of putting a stop to the two causes of these problems: humans feeding the bears and bears foraging in open garbage dumps. That strict management program continues today and visitors generally won't see any roadside bears. The magnificent animals can still be seen in the region, but usually only at a distance in the early morning or late evening when the bears are near the wooded edges of clearings.

For those bears that continue to earn the label of "problem" animals, research is underway into the possibility of modifying their behavior through aversive conditioning. These bears, when consistently involved in potentially troublesome activities, are shot at with a projectile filled with water that explodes on contact, much like a large water

Above: *Towering flames could be seen from many miles away, and smoke shrouded parts of the region like fog.* Opposite: *Although pictures like this one give the impression that the park was devastated by the fire, the real damage was much less extensive than most reports.*

This page: *Yellowstone has blossomed in the wake of the fires. The first of these photos was taken near Tower in the fall of 1988, immediately after the fires, while the second photograph shows the lush vegetation already springing forth the following summer.*

This page: *A stand of aspen near Tower shows the immediate impact of the fire that burned through this area, but new growth sprang up from the ashes the next year.*

balloon. The exploding projectile causes some pain and alarm without inflicting any real injury.

Although the large animals of the parks are truly wild creatures, many visitors view their apparently docile behavior as indications that they are tame animals, incapable of harming humans. Pamphlets handed to visitors at the parks' entrances warn of the danger of approaching such animals as buffalo, which can weigh 2,000 pounds and sprint at 30 miles per hour—three times faster than the average human can run. The same warning can justifiably be applied to almost all of the large animals in the two parks.

Although mountain lions have been documented as inhabiting the region, no such warnings are needed concerning the big cats. Only a very few lucky visitors have even caught a glimpse of the cats, much less been imperiled by them. At least 22 of the felines inhabit the northern part of Yellowstone, according to an estimate from a five-year study begun in 1987.

The only large North American mammal missing from the region is the wolf. Although the gray wolf had occupied a space at the top of the food chain for centuries, it was wiped out in the region in the early 1900's as part of a government-sponsored predator control program.

At sunset, a lone canoe glides through Oxbow Bend on the Snake River in Grand Teton National Park. Snake River cutthroat trout—a distinct subspecies of the cutthroat—depend for their survival upon the 27 miles of the river that are protected within the park.

Towering more than a mile above the floor of the valley known as Jackson Hole, seven Teton mountain peaks stand more than 12,000 feet above sea level. Below: The peaks of the uppermost Tetons are regularly shrouded in clouds. Mount Moran, which appears to rise near the banks of the Snake River, is actually more than 12 miles away.

This vacancy is in conflict with the 1973 master plan of the park, which calls for the perpetuation of the park's natural ecosystem. A movement to restore a small, experimental population of the canines into Yellowstone—supported by seven of every eight Yellowstone visitors polled—would fulfill the demands of that plan. However, ranching interests and congressional members from the region have stymied action.

Similarly controversial were the fires in the summer of 1988. The face of the wilderness region was drastically changed as wildfires burned through nearly half of Yellowstone's 2.2 million acres, 1.4 million acres all told in the overall region. More than 25,000 firefighters were brought into the fray and more than $120 million was spent on fire suppression efforts.

The National Park Service's 16-year-old policy of allowing lightning-caused fires to burn naturally was widely criticized. Daily media reports told the world that its oldest national park was being destroyed.

Only after the smoke had cleared and much of the sensationalized attention had shifted away from the park did the truth begin to emerge: Yellowstone was not completely incinerated. The wildfires had followed their natural course of burning in a

This page, top to bottom: *A dozen glaciers exist amid the towering peaks of the Tetons. Teton Glacier lies between Grand Teton (elevation 13,770 feet above sea level) and Mount Owen (elevation 12,928 feet above sea level.) Middle Teton (elevation 12,804 feet above sea level) rises above Amphitheater Lake, one of the many small bodies of water that fill the gouges created in the earth by the last Ice Age.*

Below: *Jenny Lake was created by a natural dam formed by the immense volume of rock the glaciers dumped as they retreated at the end of the last Ice Age. Mount Moran is in the distance.* Opposite: *Much of the Teton Range came under federal protection as a national park in 1929, but the lower elevations of Jackson Hole were not added until 1950.*

patchwork pattern. Immense sections of woodland remained untouched. Only 345 elk, 36 mule deer, 12 moose, 12 black bears, and nine bison were found dead in the wake of the fires.

As it had for centuries untold, the natural progression of life responded to the fires. The fires released immense amounts of nutrients back into the earth and increased sunlight penetration to the forest floor. Incredibly lush and diverse plant growth — including artwork-like conglomerations of wildflowers — have resulted. The charismatic megafauna is likewise flourishing amid the abundance of nutritive forage that's been released from the largely inedible trees. The forest is regenerating itself with new growth that would not have been possible without the fires. The wildlife is responding to new opportunities in the environment.

As this natural progression continues, the region may become an even more fascinating treat for visitors — if it's possible to top what Yellowstone and Grand Teton national parks already have to offer.

This page, top to bottom: *Services, including wedding ceremonies, are held from the spring through the fall (until snow closes the road) each year in the Chapel of the Transfiguration, which is owned by the Episcopal church. An old cabin offers a fantastic panorama of the Teton Range in the distance. Ranches, both working and tourist, are located throughout the Teton area.* Opposite: *No visitor ever forgets the commanding presence of the Tetons, but Grand Teton National Park offers a great deal at its lower elevations as well.* Overleaf: *Teton Village is a resort community nestled into the base of Rendezvous Mountain. An aerial tram transverses the distance from the town to the top of the mountain, 10,552 feet above sea level.*

Index of Photography

All photographs courtesy of The Image Bank, except where indicated*.